froglets
Learners

Volcanoes

by Annabelle Lynch

W
FRANKLIN WATTS
LONDON•SYDNEY

First published in 2014 by
Franklin Watts
338 Euston Road
London NW1 3BH

Franklin Watts Australia
Level 17/207 Kent Street
Sydney NSW 2000

Picture credits: Karl Anthony/Shutterstock: 15.
Beboy/Shutterstock: front cover, 4-5. David Clegg/
Eye Ubiquitous/Alamy: 21. Robert Crow/
Shutterstock: 10. Corey A Ford.Dreamstime: 8-9.
Pablo Hidalgo/Shutterstock: 6-7. Lauren Orr/
Shutterstock: 18. Skyearth/Shutterstock: 1, 12-13.
Nickolay Stanev/Shutterstock: 11. Lucarelli
Temistocle/Shutterstock: 16-17.

Every attempt has been made to clear copyright.
Should there be any inadvertent omission please
apply to the publisher for rectification.

A CIP catalogue record for this book is
available from the British Library.

Dewey number: 550

ISBN 978 1 4451 2913 6 (hbk)
ISBN 978 1 4451 3047 7 (pbk)
Library eBook ISBN 978 1 4451 2919 8

Series Editor: Julia Bird
Series Advisor: Catherine Glavina
Series Designer: Peter Scoulding

Printed in China

Franklin Watts is a division of Hachette Children's Books,
an Hachette UK company. www.hachette.co.uk

Contents

The words in **bold** can be found in the glossary.

What is a volcano?

Hot, runny rock called magma is found deep inside the Earth. In some places, the magma can come out. These places are called volcanoes.

Volcanoes can be found deep under the sea.

Eruption!

When magma comes out of a volcano, it is called an eruption. Eruptions happen when **pressure** builds up deep inside the Earth.

As well as magma, hot **ash** also comes out of a volcano when it erupts.

Parts of a volcano

All volcanoes have the same main parts. These include a **crater** at the top, sides or flanks, a long **vent** and a **chamber** where the magma is stored.

During an eruption, magma goes up the volcano's vent and shoots out of the crater.

Crater

Vent

Chamber

Lava and ash

Once magma is outside a volcano, it is called lava.

The lava and ash cool and get
hard. They build up the sides
of the volcano, making it
grow taller.

Lava can get as
hot as 1200°C.

Composite volcanoes

Composite volcanoes erupt quickly, shooting lava, ash and mud high into the air.

Volcanoes are different shapes and sizes. A composite volcano looks like a cone with steep sides. It is made of ash and lava.

Shield

volcanoes

Shield volcanoes are shaped like a shield or an upside-down bowl. They have sloping sides made of lava.

15

Shield volcanoes erupt slowly and gently, spilling out lava and a little ash.

Vesuvius

A volcano called Vesuvius erupted in Italy thousands of years ago.

Vesuvius last erupted in 1944, but it could erupt again any day.

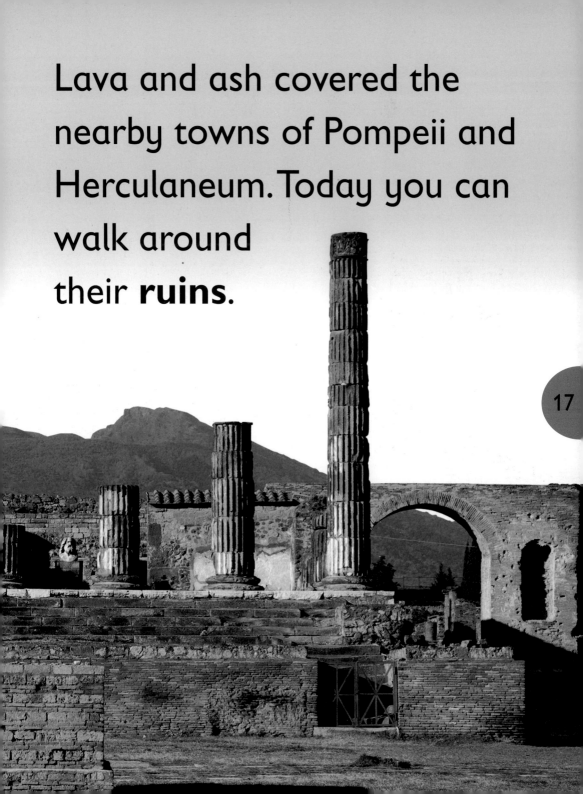

Lava and ash covered the nearby towns of Pompeii and Herculaneum. Today you can walk around their **ruins**.

Active or extinct?

Active volcanoes can erupt at any time. Dormant volcanoes have not erupted for a long time, but could erupt one day. Extinct volcanoes will not erupt again.

A volcano is active if it has erupted in the last 10,000 years.

Living with volcanoes

Millions of people around the world live close to a volcano. Lava and ash make the soil around a volcano **fertile** for growing crops.

There are around 1,500 active volcanoes in the world today.

Glossary

ash – grey or black powder

chamber – a space

crater – the hole at the top of a volcano

fertile – good land for growing plants in

pressure – when something is pushed or pressed

ruins – the parts of a building that are still standing when the rest of it has fallen down

vent – a long, narrow opening

Websites:

http://ngkids.co.uk/did-you-know/Volcano_Facts

http://www.nhm.ac.uk/kids-only/earth-space/volcanoes/

Every effort has been made by the Publishers to ensure that the websites are suitable for children, and that they contain no inappropriate or offensive material. However, because of the nature of the Internet, it is impossible to guarantee that the contents of these sites will not be altered. We strongly advise that Internet access is supervised by a responsible adult.

Quiz

1. What is magma?

2. What is it called when magma comes out of a volcano?

3. What does a composite volcano look like?

4. Where is Vesuvius?

5. What is an extinct volcano?

6. How many active volcanoes are there in the world?

The answers are on page 24

Answers

1. Hot, runny rock
2. An eruption
3. A cone with steep sides
4. In Italy
5. A volcano that will not erupt again
6. Around 1,500

Index

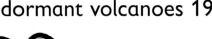